A BRIEF ILLUSTRATED
HISTORY of
SCIENCE

JOHN MALAM
&
DAVID WEST

raintree

a Capstone company — publishers for children

Published by Raintree, an imprint of Capstone Global Library Limited, 2017.
Raintree is an imprint of Capstone Global Library Limited, a company incorporated in England and Wales having its registered office at 264 Banbury Road, Oxford, OX2 7DY -
Registered company number: 6695582
www.raintree.co.uk
myorders@raintree.co.uk

Designed and illustrated by David West
Text by John Malam
Editor Brenda Haugen
Produced by
David West Children's Books, 6 Princeton Court, 55 Felsham Road, London SW15 1AZ
Printed and bound in China

ISBN: 978-1-4747-2704-4 (hardcover)
20 19 18 17 16
10 9 8 7 6 5 4 3 2 1

British Library Cataloguing in Publication Data
A full catalogue record for this book is available from the British Library.

Every effort has been made to contact copyright holders of material reproduced in this book. Any omissions will be rectified in subsequent printings if notice is given to the publisher.

Photographic credits: Page 4, Photograph by Rama, Wikimedia Commons, Cc-by-sa-2.0-fr; page 26, 1997-2016 CERN

CONTENTS

INTRODUCTION

Socrates (470–399 BCE) of ancient Greece suggested ways to investigate problems and increase knowledge that are still used today.

SCIENCE IS VAST AND COMPLEX. THERE ARE HUNDREDS OF BRANCHES, FROM ASTRONOMY TO ZOOLOGY. At its simplest, science is the search for knowledge and understanding. It tries to find answers to questions such as what, where, when, why and how? It also uses this information in practical ways, often to help in daily life.

Practical science goes back thousands of years, with activities such as farming, building the first cities, predicting events using calendars and inventing the wheel. From about 3,500 years ago, ancient Greeks began to think about the ideas and laws behind these practical activities and how and why things happen. The scientific method – asking a question, doing tests and experiments, studying the results and adding to scientific knowledge – began around 500 years ago. Today science is everywhere, from the innermost parts of an atom, to communications, construction, transport, leisure time, food, medicine, the natural world, climate change, space and studying the origin and fate of the Universe.

Farming as science

From about 12,000 years ago, people began to settle down, plant crops and keep animals rather than wandering as hunter-gatherers. They tested different varieties of crops and livestock and bred the best ones to improve the amounts of food. These early farmers, as in ancient Egypt (right), were in effect carrying out scientific experiments.

Early surgery

Various ancient peoples drilled holes in the skulls of living patients (below), perhaps trying to let out 'evil spirits' that were causing pain or strange behaviour.

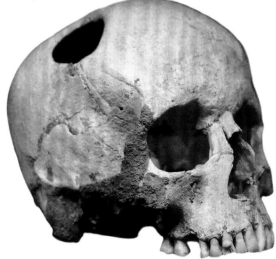

Early astronomy

For 6,000 years people have kept records of the Sun, Moon and stars, sometimes building great stone structures to help their observations (right). These became early calendars to predict important events like seasonal floods and eclipses.

NATURAL PHILOSOPHERS
SCIENCE OF THE ANCIENT SCHOLARS

Modern science can trace its origins back to ancient times, when the search for knowledge and an understanding of the world began. Nowhere was this more apparent than in the world of the ancient Greeks, who lived around the shores of the Mediterranean and Aegean seas.

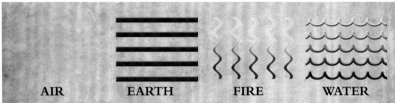

| AIR | EARTH | FIRE | WATER |

Empedocles originated the theory of the four classical elements.

The four elements

The ancient Greeks wanted to understand the world around them. Empedocles was a philosopher from a Greek city on the island of Sicily. In the 5th century BCE, Empedocles said that everything was made up of a mixture of four basic elements – air, earth, fire and water. To prove it, he carried out a simple experiment. He set light to a stick. Because the stick burned, it obviously contained fire. As it burned, the stick gave off smoke, which showed it contained air. When the fire was out, a black, dirty residue was left behind, so the stick must contain earth. Because the residue was damp, water must also be present. The idea that all things were made of these four elements lasted for about 2,000 years.

Geocentric orbit shows Earth at the centre with the planets and the Sun orbiting it.

In the third century BCE, Aristarchus of Samos was the first to suggest Earth and the other planets orbited the Sun.

Astronomy

Astronomy was pioneered by the ancient Greeks. They catalogued about 850 stars and identified five of the planets (besides Earth). The planets they observed were: Mercury, Venus, Mars, Jupiter and Saturn. They believed, wrongly, that Earth was at the centre of the solar system, and the planets and Sun moved around it in circles. However, in about 275 BCE, Aristarchus of Samos said the opposite. He claimed the Sun was at the centre, and the planets revolved around it.

In about AD 135, Claudius Ptolemy of Alexandria, the greatest astronomer of the time, wrote a book that put Earth at the centre. It became the standard astronomy text for the next 1,400 years.

Mathematics

The study of mathematics was one of the greatest achievements of the ancient Greeks. By about 500 BCE, Pythagoras had discovered a basic rule of geometry. Named Pythagoras's theorem after him,

Pythagoras's theorem states that the square of the hypotenuse (C) in a right-angled triangle is equal to the sum of the squares of the other two sides.

$$A^2+B^2=C^2$$

Euclid compiled a 13-book reference guide to mathematics and geometry called Elements.

it can be used to calculate the length of any of the sides of a right-angled triangle or the distance between two points

Ancient Greek mathematicians wrote textbooks, and in the 200s BCE, Euclid's *Elements* brought together all that was known at the time about mathematics. The book became a standard maths textbook for students until modern times.

Archimedes

Of all the mathematicians of ancient Greece, Archimedes was among the greatest. He spent his life studying geometry, particularly circles, spheres and spirals. He was also an inventor who developed new machines, such as giant cranes that could lift enemy ships out of the water, and large mirrors that focused the Sun's rays on ships to set them on fire. His best known invention was a water pump – the Archimedes's screw – which raised water from a low level to a high level. Farmers used it to water their crops.

Archimedes demonstrates his machine, a tube with an internal screw that raised water, since known as the 'Archimedes's screw'.

Mapping the world

In their quest for knowledge, the ancient Greeks produced some of the first maps of the world. In the 500s BCE, Anaximander created a map of all known land, which he placed around the Aegean Sea. His map became the base map which others added to and improved as the Greeks learned more about geography. Three hundred years after Anaximander's map, Eratosthenes created a map of the Mediterranean region, showing Europe, North Africa and Asia.

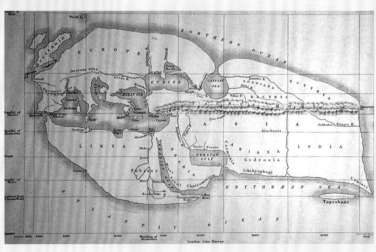

19th-century reconstruction of Eratosthenes's map of the world, around 194 BCE

Claudius Ptolemy (AD 100–170) was a mathematician, an astronomer, geographer and astrologer who lived and worked in Alexandria, Egypt.

EARLY MEDICINE
AND THE NATURAL WORLD

Good science depends on careful, accurate observation and the conducting of experiments. The ancient Greeks came to realise this, and in so doing laid the foundations for the proper study of science. This was most keenly seen in medicine, where scientific methods slowly replaced old beliefs and practices in magic.

Hippocrates (460–370 BCE) is referred to as the 'Father of Western Medicine'.

From magic to medicine

By the 5th century BCE, there was a belief in ancient Greece in 'temple medicine'. The sick would sleep in temples dedicated to the god Asclepius, hoping he would appear in a dream and reveal how they were to be healed. This was magic, not medicine.

Ideas changed when Greek doctors decided that bad body fluids were the cause of illness. By taking a person's blood, they believed they were removing bad fluid and that the person would recover. In the 400s BCE, Hippocrates set up a school of medicine, where observation, diagnosis and treatment replaced magic. The science of medicine had begun.

Temples dedicated to the healer-god Asclepius functioned as centres of medical diagnosis and healing.

The natural world

A scientist, philosopher and teacher, Aristotle was one of the ancient world's greatest thinkers. He lived in ancient Greece in the 300s BCE. His curiosity led him to establish systems of classifying and describing the natural world. He created new branches of science, including biology (the study of living organisms), zoology (the study of the behaviour of animals) and physics (the science of matter and energy). Aristotle also separated science from philosophy, setting it on its future course of learning through observation and experiments. Much of his writing, and that of other Greek and Roman scientists, survived, leading to the rebirth of scientific study in the Renaissance in the AD 1300s.

Aristotle is the earliest natural historian whose work has survived in some detail.

Theophrastus's two surviving botanical works, Enquiry into Plants *and* On the Causes of Plants, *were an important influence on European Renaissance science.*

Anatomy

Key to the treatment of illness and disease was an understanding of anatomy – the structure of the human body, particularly the skeleton and the circulatory system of vessels that carry blood. There was also a quest to find the body's 'command centre', with

Erasistratus takes the pulse of a patient. Along with fellow physician Herophilus, he founded a school of anatomy in Alexandria, where they researched how the body was made up.

opinions divided between the brain, the heart and the liver.

Galen of Pergamon

Born in Pergamon, a Greek city in present-day Turkey, Galen was one of the ancient world's most important writers on medicine. He studied human anatomy at medical school in Alexandria, Egypt, but he never dissected a human body. Instead, he cut up the bodies of monkeys, thinking they were the same as human bodies on the inside. Galen's reputation grew, and he moved to Rome where he was doctor to four Roman emperors.

Galen wrote about the human body and medicine, especially anatomy, muscles, bones and the treatment of illness. His books were the main source of medical knowledge in the Western world for the next 1,400 years.

Roman surgical tools found at Pompeii (right)

Galen treated gladiators' wounds, referring to them as 'windows into the body'.

Pliny the Elder

Writer and cavalry commander, Gaius Plinius Secundus (known as Pliny the Elder) compiled the Roman world's most important encyclopedia. His *Natural History* recorded more than 20,000 facts about the Universe, geography, zoology, botany, medicine, art, architecture, minerology and the human race. Pliny's great work has preserved knowledge from the ancient world that would otherwise have been lost and unknown to us.

Pliny wrote an encyclopedic work, Naturalis Historia *(Natural History). He died on 25 August, AD 79, during the eruption of Vesuvius.*

MEDIEVAL SCIENCE
THE ISLAMIC GOLDEN AGE

D URING A CREATIVE PERIOD THAT LASTED 300 YEARS, KNOWN AS THE ISLAMIC GOLDEN AGE (ROUGHLY AD 750–1050), ARAB SCHOLARS MADE MANY SCIENTIFIC AND MEDICAL DISCOVERIES. THEY TRANSLATED THE WORKS OF GREEK AND ROMAN WRITERS INTO ARABIC, PRESERVING THESE ANCIENT TEXTS FOR THE FUTURE IN MAJOR LIBRARIES IN BAGHDAD, CAIRO AND DAMASCUS.

Rhazes's books were standard texts for Islamic and European medical students for centuries.

Medicine and human anatomy

Abu Bakr Mohammad Ibn Zakariya al-Razi (known in the West as Rhazes) was the leading scholar of the early Islamic world. He was director of a hospital in Baghdad, in present-day Iraq, and saw the importance of making notes about the progress and symptoms of illnesses. He correctly saw that measles and smallpox were different diseases, not the same disease with different rashes.

Another great Arab scholar was Hunain ibn Ishaq, who translated ancient Greek medical texts into Arabic and was interested in the workings of the eye.

the eye according to Hunain ibn Ishaq (right)

This illustration, from a Western translation of Alhazen's Book of Optics, *shows how sunlight reflected from a mirror on the land could be used as a weapon to set fire to ships.*

Alhazen's *Book of Optics*

Born in present-day Iraq in AD 965, Al-Hasan Ibn al-Haytham (known in the West as Alhazen) explained the nature of light and vision. He used a dark chamber he called 'Albeit Almuzlim', known today as the 'camera obscura' – the device that forms the basis of photography. Alhazen carried out experiments to test his theories about light, and how the eyes see, which he described in many books, the greatest of which is his *Book of Optics*. In this book he overturned old ideas put forward by the ancient Greeks and Romans, that said rays of light came from the eyes. Alhazen said, correctly, that vision takes place by light entering the eye. He gave names to several parts of the eye, such as the lens, the retina and the cornea. Today, Alhazen is widely considered to be the 'Father of Modern Optics'.

From alchemy to chemistry

Arab scholars were interested in a branch of science they referred to as 'al-kimiya', from which comes the English word 'alchemy'. At the time, alchemy was the scientific study of how substances could be changed or made into other substances. Through their work, Arab alchemists discovered many important substances, including hydrochloric acid, sulphuric acid, nitric acid, soda and potassium. The words they used to describe the substances they worked with have become part of everyday modern science, such as alkali (from the Arabic al-qali) and alcohol (from al-kohl), where the word al- means 'the'. As for

Al-Azhar university in Cairo, Egypt

the Arabic al-kimiya, there is no simple translation, as the word kimiya may go back to the ancient Egyptian word kemet (for 'black', in reference to the colour of Egypt's fertile soil), which then passed to the ancient Greeks, and eventually to the Arabs. What is clear, though, is that from the Arabic word kimiya comes the word 'chemistry'.

Among the great Arab chemists was Jabir ibn Hayyan, sometimes referred to as the 'Father of Chemistry'. Working in the AD 700s, Jabir was the first to suggest that chemical elements were made of small particles invisible to the naked eye. He laid the groundwork for what is known today as the periodic table of elements.

Jabir ibn Hayyan, called Gerber in the West, teaching in the school of Edesa (left)

The Istanbul Observatory

In 1571 Taqi ad-Din, known as al-Rasid (the observer), was made chief astronomer to the Ottoman court, based in Istanbul, in present-day Turkey. Six years later, in 1577, the famous Istanbul Observatory was opened. From there, Taqi ad-Din observed the night sky. He tracked the movements of the planets, Sun and Moon and produced accurate astronomical tables that replaced old, outdated ones. After only three years, the observatory was destroyed, by people who were opposed to it and who had little interest in science.

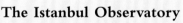

Taqi ad-Din invented a framed sextant, used to measure distances between the stars.

The Istanbul Observatory was one of the largest observatories in the Islamic world, with a staff of 16 people – eight observers, four clerks and four assistants.

MEDIEVAL SCIENCE
IN EUROPE

Starting in the 1300s, countries in western Europe began coming out of the Middle Ages, as artists, architects, scientists and educated people challenged old ideas and made new discoveries. The period is called the Renaissance, which means 'rebirth'.

Toward understanding the body

Like their counterparts in ancient Greece and Rome, some 1,500 years before them, scholars in medieval Europe wanted to understand the human body. This meant opening the body up – dissecting it – something that ancient doctors, such as Galen, never did. In 1521, Jacopo Berengario, a surgeon from Italy, wrote a book that contained the first detailed illustrations of the human body, showing the skeleton, muscles and internal organs.

Later in the 1500s, a Flemish anatomist, Andreas Vesalius, corrected errors about the body that had lasted from ancient times. For this he is thought of as the 'Father of Anatomy'.

Andreas Vesalius's, On the Fabric of the Human Body, *published in 1543, was a major advance in the study of human anatomy.*

Jacopo Berengario (above, centre) claimed to have dissected hundreds of bodies and was the most important anatomist before Andreas Vesalius.

Roger Bacon was one of the earliest European advocates of the modern scientific method inspired by Aristotle and by later scholars such as the Arab scientist Alhazen.

Universities and learning

For the first few hundred years of the medieval period in Europe, Christian cathedral schools and monasteries were the places where learning and teaching took place. Then, in the 11th century, a new type of educational institution appeared – the university. The first was in Bologna, Italy (1088), followed by Oxford, England (around 1096). Scholars at universities searched for knowledge, particularly in the arts, religion, law and medicine.

a university class in the 1350s

translating scholarly works into Latin

Roger Bacon

An English philosopher, scholar, scientist and monk, Roger Bacon insisted on the importance of scientific observation and experiments. He had a questioning mind, and investigated sight and the passage of light through lenses, leading to the development of glasses. Bacon included many of his observations in his greatest book, *Opus Maius*. Written at the request of Pope Clement IV, in Latin, Bacon's *Opus Maius* was an encyclopedia of science with sections on optics, mathematics, alchemy and astronomy.

Nicolas Copernicus and astronomy

Ever since ancient times, it was believed that Earth was at the centre of the solar system and the other planets and Sun moved around it in circles. This age-old belief was overturned by Polish astronomer Nicolas Copernicus, who worked out, correctly, that the Sun is at the centre and Earth and the other planets move around it. This was a new concept, which Copernicus described in a book that came out in 1543.

Eilmer of Malmesbury, an 11th-century English Benedictine monk, was one of the first people on record to attempt gliding flight. He failed and broke his legs, which left him lame for the rest of his life.

The work of Nicolas Copernicus in the 1500s marked the beginning of modern astronomy.

Gutenberg and the printing press

In around 1439 in Germany, Johannes Gutenberg discovered a method of printing that used individual metal letters. The letters could be arranged into words, fixed into a frame to hold them tight, then coated with a thin layer of ink. When the inked letters were pressed onto a sheet of paper by a machine, they made an inky impression, and a page of a book had been printed. The process could be repeated again and again, making multiple identical copies. Gutenberg's printing process meant that for the first time in Europe, books could be printed quickly and cheaply, helping to spread ideas and information. By 1500, there were printing presses working throughout Europe. It is often said that the medieval world in Europe ended with the introduction of the printing press.

Johannes Gutenberg's printing press played a key role in the development of the scientific revolution.

THE SCIENTIFIC REVOLUTION
OPTICS AND TIMEPIECES

WITH IMPROVEMENTS IN MAKING LENSES, SCIENTISTS COULD FOR THE FIRST TIME SEE OBJECTS TOO FAR AWAY OR TOO SMALL FOR THE HUMAN EYE. FITTED TO TELESCOPES AND MICROSCOPES, STRONGER LENSES ALLOWED NEW WORLDS TO BE VIEWED, CHALLENGING OLD IDEAS AND RAISING NEW QUESTIONS FOR SCIENCE TO CONSIDER.

Tycho Brahe was the last major astronomer to work without the aid of a telescope.

Seeing with the eye

Danish astronomer Tycho Brahe built an observatory on the island of Hven, between Denmark and Sweden in 1576. He made what were at the time the most accurate measurements for the positions of stars and planets. Brahe made his observations with the naked eye, working before the invention of the telescope. After Brahe's death, Johannes Kepler, his German assistant, continued his work. Kepler determined that the planets move around the Sun in oval orbits, not circles as had always been thought.

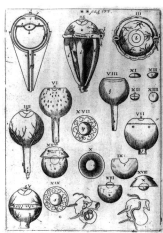

a plate from Kepler's The Optical Part of Astronomy, *illustrating the structure of eyes*

Seeing farther with a telescope

In 1609 Italian astronomer Galileo Galilei heard about the invention of the telescope in Holland. He made one for himself, pointed it up to the night sky and became the first person to observe the Moon and planets with a telescope. Like Nicolas Copernicus before him, Galileo became convinced that the Sun was at the centre of the solar system, not Earth. It was a daring idea because it went against the view of the Catholic Church, which put him under house arrest and tried to make him change his mind.

Galileo, standing, demonstrates his telescope.

The first microscopes

The 17th century saw the development of the first microscopes – instruments that used lenses to magnify an object many times over, making it visible to the human eye. Anton van Leeuwenhoek, in Holland, became the first person to observe bacteria. His microscope used a single lens. English physicist Robert Hooke improved the microscope by fitting it with several lenses. He published the first detailed illustrations of what he had seen, such as the stinging hairs on a nettle leaf and a close-up view of a flea.

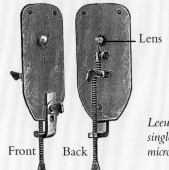

Lens

Leeuwenhoek's single-lens microscope

Front   Back

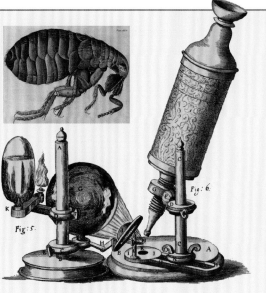

Hooke's microscope with one of his drawings of a flea

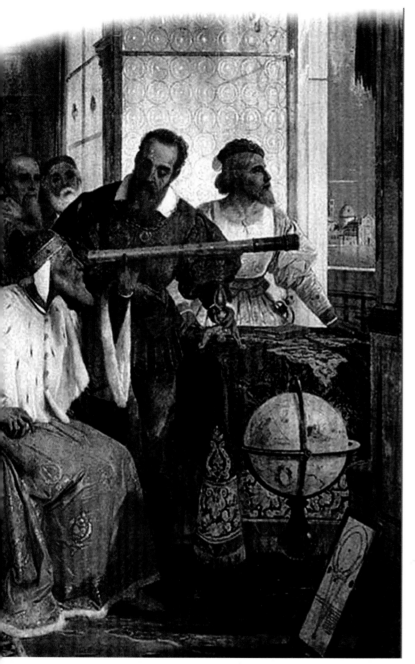

Galileo's discoveries

Through his use of a telescope, Galileo discovered craters on the Moon, spots on the Sun (sunspots), rings around Saturn and four of Jupiter's moons.

Stars and comets

By the time of English astronomer Edmond Halley (1656–1742), the positions of many stars in the northern sky were well known. But the positions of stars in the southern sky were a mystery. In 1678, after studying the stars in the Southern Hemisphere for two years, Halley published the first book to describe them, listing a total of 341 stars.

Halley was also interested in comets – icy objects, often with tails of gas, that orbit the Sun. He found that comets travel on fixed routes and return at regular intervals. Halley predicted that the same bright comet seen every 75 or 76 years (1531, 1607, 1682) would next be seen in 1758, which it was.

The comet observed by Edmond Halley is named in his honour. Halley's Comet is the most famous of all the comets and will next be visible in 2061.

Halley's map of the path of the solar eclipse across England in in 1715

Improved timekeeping

With the invention of the pendulum (swinging weight) clock by Christiaan Huygens in 1656,

time could be measured with greater accuracy than ever before. The Dutch mathematician and astronomer discovered that a swinging pendulum keeps regular time and could therefore be used as a regulator for clocks. Until then, clocks used coiled springs, but as they unwound they lost time, which could be about 15 minutes a day. Huygens's pendulum clock only lost about 15 seconds per day. Better timekeeping saw clockmakers fit minute hands to clock faces, from around 1690. Before then, most clocks simply had an hour hand.

Christiaan Huygens (1629–1695)

the workings of the pendulum clock from Horologium Oscillatorium *(1658) by Huygens*

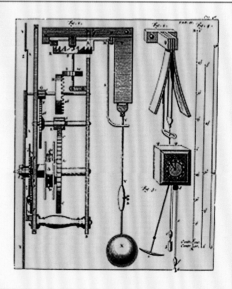

THE SCIENTIFIC REVOLUTION
ISAAC NEWTON

T HE DISCOVERIES MADE IN THE 17TH CENTURY BY ENGLISH SCIENTIST ISAAC NEWTON REVOLUTIONISED SCIENCE. HE DEVELOPED THE LAW OF GRAVITY AND THE THREE LAWS OF MOTION (WHICH BECAME THE BASIS FOR PHYSICS), INVENTED A NEW TYPE OF TELESCOPE AND FOUND THAT WHITE LIGHT WAS MADE UP OF DIFFERENT COLOURS.

Newton's theory of colour

Before Newton, telescopes used clear glass lenses, and when a bright object was viewed it appeared with a mysterious coloured edge around it. Newton suspected the colour had something to do with light itself, and he discovered that white light is a mixture of all the colours (red, orange, yellow, green, blue, indigo and violet). He proved this by passing a beam of light through a prism, which refracted (bent) the light. When the light left the prism, it was broken down into its seven colours.

Newton realised that a clear telescope lens was splitting white light into its colours, and that led him to develop the reflecting or mirror telescope, which gave images with no coloured edges.

Newton's reflecting telescope used mirrors to give clear images.

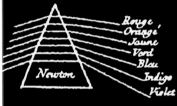

Newton demonstrated that white light is made up of a multicoloured spectrum when bent by a prism.

Laws of motion and gravity

When Newton saw an apple fall out of a tree to the ground, he wondered what had made it fall straight down. Newton was the first to realise that, just as the force of gravity had caused the apple to fall, gravity must exist throughout the whole Universe. According to Newton, the force of gravity kept the Moon in orbit around Earth, and the planets in orbit around the Sun.

Newton described his theory of gravity in 1687, in his book *Principia*, one of the most important scientific books ever written. In the same book, Newton described the three laws of motion, which state how an object moves and what forces act upon it. To explain his revolutionary new theories, Newton invented a new kind of mathematics, called calculus, with which to express the laws of motion. Newton's work continues to influence science today.

Principia (Mathematical Principles of Natural Philosophy) stated Newton's three laws of motion and the law of universal gravitation.

PHILOSOPHIÆ
NATURALIS
PRINCIPIA
MATHEMATICA.

Autore JS. NEWTON, Trin. Coll. Cantab. Soc. Mathefeos Profeffore Lucafiano, & Societatis Regalis Sodali.

IMPRIMATUR
S. PEPYS, Reg. Soc. PRÆSES.
Julii 5. 1686.

LONDINI,
Juffu Societatis Regiæ ac Typis Jofephi Streater. Proftat apud plures Bibliopolas. Anno MDCLXXXVII.

THE SCIENTIFIC REVOLUTION
SCIENTIFIC METHOD

For scientists, it's all-important to be able to repeat an experiment or confirm an observation or a calculation. This process of checking and testing started to become the correct scientific method in the 1600s, slowly overturning centuries of old-fashioned unscientific ideas.

Francis Bacon

Francis Bacon's scientific method

Although Francis Bacon was not a scientist (he was an English statesman and writer), he was a leading figure in the development of scientific method in the early 1600s. Bacon firmly believed that by collecting and examining all known facts from experiments and observations (rather than by using logic-based arguments as natural philosophers had done), the laws of science would be discovered. The Baconian method sparked a wave of new scientific discoveries.

Robert Boyle demonstrates his air pump and the effect on a bird when the air is pumped out of the jar.

Robert Boyle

One of the first to adopt the new method of scientific enquiry was Irish scientist Robert Boyle. He carried out controlled experiments and published his findings with details of his method and the equipment he used. It meant other scientists could repeat Boyle's experiments to check his results.

Torricelli invented the barometer in 1642 by inverting a tube filled with mercury into a bowl of mercury. A vacuum, created at the top of the tube, varied according to air pressure.

Magnetic Earth

Sailors had known for centuries that a compass needle always points to the north, but they had no idea why. The mystery was solved in 1600 by William Gilbert, an English scientist.

William Gilbert demonstrated his experiments with magnets to Queen Elizabeth I of England.

He determined that Earth has an iron core. The core creates a magnetic field around the planet, with magnetic north and south poles. This explained why a compass needle would always be attracted to Earth's magnetic North Pole.

An old Earth

In the 1700s, James Hutton, a Scottish scientist, wondered why fossilised shells were found high up on mountains, far fom the sea. He realised that rocks are a record of

Earth's distant past, being lifted up from deep inside the planet, before being slowly eroded down, in a process now called the 'rock cycle'. He reasoned that for this to happen the planet must be millions of years old, not thousands as was thought.

James Hutton's pioneering work in the study of rocks around the coast of Scotland established geology as a science in its own right.

AGE OF ENLIGHTENMENT
1715 – 1815

AN OPEN-MINDED MOVEMENT SWEPT ACROSS EUROPE IN THE 18TH CENTURY, GIVING PEOPLE THE COURAGE TO THINK AND SPEAK FOR THEMSELVES, RATHER THAN AUTOMATICALLY BELIEVING WHAT THEY HAD BEEN TOLD. THIS WAS THE AGE OF ENLIGHTENMENT, WHICH CAME AT A TIME WHEN SCIENTISTS AND INVENTORS WERE CHALLENGING OLD BELIEFS, AND MAKING IMPORTANT DISCOVERIES.

Joseph Black (1728–1799)

British scientists and inventors developed the steam engine. Joseph Black was among the first to experiment with steam. Thomas Newcomen developed the first working steam engine (1712), which James Watt improved in the 1770s (right).

The power of steam

The 18th century was a time of great technical progress, referred to as the Industrial Revolution. At the forefront of the new technology in transforming industry was steam power. Coal was burned to heat water in a boiler (a metal cylinder), and the steam that was given off was used to power machines, known as steam engines. The first steam engines were immobile machines, pumping water out of mines and powering machinery in textile mills. By the early 1800s, steam was being used to power locomotives – machines that moved along iron rails. They were the world's first railway engines.

Improvements in boiler technology led to high-pressure steam engines and the first steam locomotives, such as Richard Trevithick's locomotive of 1802.

William and Caroline Herschel grind and polish a glass lens for their reflecting telescope.

The Herschels

German brother and sister William and Caroline Herschel were astronomers working in England. In 1781 William discovered Uranus, the first new planet found since ancient times and the first to be discovered with a telescope.

Vaccination, a medical milestone

Smallpox was a deadly disease with no known cure. In 1796 Edward Jenner, an English doctor, discovered how to protect people from catching it by injecting them with a mild infection passed to humans by cows. Jenner had discovered vaccination, a major advance in protecting lives.

James Phipps, 8, was the first to be vaccinated.

Electricity – power of the future

In the United States, scientist and statesman Benjamin Franklin carried out an experiment. In 1752 he flew a kite into thunderclouds. Lightning struck the kite, and an electrical current moved down the string to a metal key. When Franklin reached out to the key, a spark jumped toward him.

Franklin concluded electricity in the clouds had caused the spark, proving that lightning was a form of electricity.

In 1799 Alessandro Volta, in Italy, invented the first battery, inside which electricity could be stored.

Benjamin Franklin (above) flew a kite to collect an electric charge from a storm cloud, proving lightning was electrical. Alessandro Volta (left) demonstrates his battery to Napoleon Bonaparte in 1801.

Dalton's atomic theory

Everything is made up of tiny particles of matter called atoms, so small they are invisible to the naked eye. It was the ancient Greeks who first came up with the idea of atoms, around 400 BCE, but it was not until the 19th century that scientists took a closer look at the building blocks of matter.

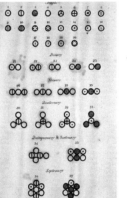

In 1808, English scientist John Dalton described the atom as the smallest particle of matter. Dalton realised that atoms in the same element are always exactly the same, and that atoms from different elements can be combined to make different chemicals.

various atoms and molecules depicted by John Dalton (above)

The chemistry of air

In France, Antoine Lavoisier wanted to improve street lighting, so he studied how various fuels burned in lamps. Through this work he realised that air contains two gases, one of which he named 'oxygen' (the other gas is nitrogen). Lavoisier named other new elements, gave more accurate names to elements that were already known, and arranged them into family groups.

French scientists also pioneered the early study of the atmosphere.

French chemist Antoine Lavoisier was assisted by his wife, Marie-Anne Pierrette Paulze.

Joseph Gay-Lussac and Jean Biot made the first scientific balloon flight in 1804, rising to 7,016 metres (23,018 feet). to investigate Earth's atmosphere.

They ascended in hot air balloons to gather information about temperature, humidity and air pressure at various heights above the ground.

THE 19TH CENTURY
THE AGE OF PROFESSIONAL SCIENCE

SCIENCE GAINED RESPECT IN THE 19TH CENTURY. GREAT ADVANCES WERE MADE IN THE FIELDS OF CHEMISTRY, PHYSICS, BIOLOGY AND MEDICINE AND, AS A RESULT, IMPROVEMENTS WERE MADE TO INDUSTRIAL PROCESSES, HEALTH AND TRANSPORT. SCIENCE MOVED AWAY FROM BEING THE WORK OF 'GENTLEMAN AMATEURS' TO AN EMERGING BODY OF PROFESSIONAL SCIENTISTS.

Jacob Berzelius (1779–1848)

Atomic chemistry

In 1789 Frenchman Antoine Lavoisier put the chemical elements into order, listing 33 substances. Englishman John Dalton increased the list to 36 elements in 1808 and proposed a symbol for each one. But Dalton's symbols were difficult to remember.

Mendeleev's periodic table

A breakthrough came in 1813, when Swedish chemist Jacob Berzelius invented a system that used letters for 47 elements, from Al (aluminium) to Zr (zirconium). The system is still used today. The next step came in 1869, when Russian chemist Dimitri Mendeleev arranged all known chemical elements (63 at the time) into a pattern called the 'periodic table'. Mendeleev organised the elements by their atomic weights, and when he had completed his table, he saw gaps. He predicted new elements would be found to fill the gaps. Mendeleev was correct, and today's periodic table has 118 elements.

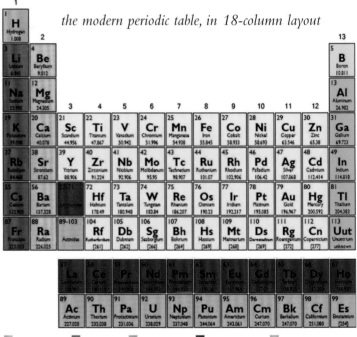

the modern periodic table, in 18-column layout

■ nonmetal ■ halogen ■ noble gas ■ lanthanide ■ actinide

Vaccination

Nineteenthth-century French scientist Louis Pasteur discovered that microscopic living organisms (bacteria) carried diseases from person to person, or from animals to humans. He found that if he gave a person a weak form of a disease, the person became immune to its stronger, dangerous form. He made vaccines against rabies and anthrax.

Pasteur also discovered that heating drinks such as wine and beer to 63°Celsius (145°Fahrenheit) killed the microorganisms that made them go sour. The process of pasteurisation that is still widely used to keep drinks and food fresh for longer is named after him.

The German doctor Robert Koch is considered the founder of modern bacteriology. His findings made a great contribution to the development of the first chemicals designed to attack specific bacteria.

Louis Pasteur (1822–1895) is famed for his process of pasteurisation.

William Ramsay's work in isolating argon, helium, neon, krypton and xenon led to the development of a new section of the periodic table.

Oil industry develops

The oil industry began in Poland with the work of Ignacy Lukasiewicz. In 1853 he invented the kerosene or paraffin lamp, which burned a fuel (kerosene) obtained by refining oil. It was a worldwide success, and the kerosene lamp soon replaced lamps that burned whale oil. The discovery that oil could be put to practical use led to the opening of the first oil refinery, in Poland, in 1856.

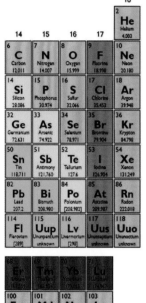

Ignacy Lukasiewicz built the world's first oil refinery in 1856.

Standard Oil Refinery No. 1 in Ohio, 1897

semi metal ■ basic metal transition metal ■ alkaline earth ■ alkali metal

Nicolas Léonard Sadi Carnot (1796–1832)

Understanding steam power

By the early 19th century, steam power had revolutionised industry, with steam engines draining water from mines, forging iron, grinding grain, and spinning and weaving cloth. But they produced very little power for the vast amounts of coal they burned. Nicolas Carnot, a French engineer, studied steam power. His work in the 1820s led to a new branch of science, thermodynamics – the study of heat and how it relates to energy.

Stephenson's steam locomotive, Rocket, *1829*

The coming of railways

The 1820s saw improvements to the steam locomotive. In 1825, British engineer George Stephenson designed the world's first passenger railway line (Stockton and Darlington railway). In 1829 his locomotive *Rocket* was chosen as the most efficient engine to run between Manchester and Liverpool.

Theory of evolution

Charles Darwin's visit to the remote Galapagos Islands in 1832 led to his theory that all animal life on Earth was as a result of evolution by natural selection. This is the idea that all species of life have evolved from common ancestors. Darwin described his idea in the book *On the Origin of Species* (1859). Alfred Russel Wallace had a similar idea at the same time as Darwin. Their theory was controversial, because it seemed to go against ideas in the Bible.

birds of paradise from Wallace's book, The Malay Archipelago

Charles Darwin (inset) started to form his theory of evolution on his voyage around the world aboard HMS Beagle *(1831–1836).*

Nineteenth-century scientists and inventors were particularly attracted to the study of the electromagnetic spectrum. Invisible waves of energy could be put to practical use, from sending messages around the world using radio waves, to seeing inside the body with X-rays.

Michael Faraday in his laboratory in the 1850s

Michael Faraday and the electrical industry

Michael Faraday, the son of an English blacksmith, was one of the 19th century's greatest practical scientists. His experiments with electricity led to important inventions. Through the work of French scientist André-Marie Ampère, Faraday knew that when electricity flowed through a coil, the coil behaved like a magnet. Faraday thought that if electricity could make a magnet, then a magnet could make electricity. He was correct, and in the 1820s and 1830s, he invented the first electric motor and electric generator. Faraday was a pioneering scientist, whose work led to the development of the worldwide electrical industry.

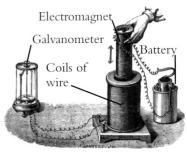

Faraday's experiment showed electromagnetic induction. When an electromagnet is moved in and out of coils of wire it induces a current that is detected by the galvanometer.

Electromagnet
Galvanometer
Battery
Coils of wire

James Clerk Maxwell and electromagnetism

In the mid-1800s, Scottish scientist James Clerk Maxwell developed a theory that light, electricity and magnetism are connected – the theory of electromagnetism. He said that light was an electromagnetic wave and that other waves existed. He was correct. After his death X-rays and other waves were discovered.

Maxwell's theory of electromagnetic waves brought together for the first time light, electricity and magnetism.

Longer wavelengths

James Clerk Maxwell   RADIO WAVES   MICROWAVES

The War of Currents

American inventor Thomas Edison invented the phonograph, which recorded the spoken voice and played it back. He was also a co-inventor of the electric light bulb. He pioneered the direct current (DC) system of electricity in the 1880s, which came under competition from the rival alternating current (AC) system of George Westinghouse. The AC system used some of inventor Nikola Tesla's ideas. Both systems competed to bring electricty into American homes and businesses, in what became known as the 'War of Currents'. The AC system won, because it was the cheaper of the two.

Thomas Edison (left) developed a system of electric power generation and distribution to homes, businesses and factories.
Nikola Tesla (below) is best known for his contributions to the design of the modern alternating current electricity supply system.

Waves and wavelengths

Maxwell's theory of electromagnetism laid the foundations for discovering the electromagnetic spectrum – the idea that electromagnetic energy travels in waves. The waves span a broad spectrum, from the very long radio waves to very short gamma rays. The wavelength is the distance between the crest of one wave crest to the next. The human eye can only see a small portion of this spectrum, called visible light. All other electromagnetic waves are invisible but can be detected by machines (a radio picks up radio waves, for example).

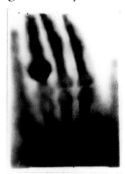

Wilhelm Röntgen's first X-ray, of his wife's left hand and wedding ring, 1895

X-rays see inside the body

One of the most important discoveries in the electromagnetic spectrum was the discovery of X-rays by German scientist Wilhelm Röntgen in 1895. He found they had so much energy, they could travel through most materials, but some were stopped by bones. By passing X-rays through the human body, Röntgen was able to take photographs of the bones inside.

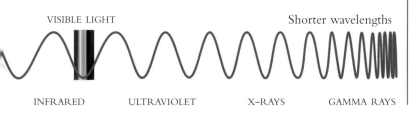

VISIBLE LIGHT   Shorter wavelengths

INFRARED   ULTRAVIOLET   X–RAYS   GAMMA RAYS

Pierre and Marie Curie in the laboratory

Discovery of radioactivity

French scientist Antoine Becquerel discovered that when the heavy metal uranium broke down, it gave off a stream of particles (alpha and beta particles). It also gave off gamma rays, which have more energy than X-rays. The stream was an electromagnetic wave, known as radiation. Becquerel's discovery of radioactivity led the husband and wife team Pierre and Marie Curie to study uranium. In 1898 they discovered the dangerous radioactive elements radium and polonium.

Antoine Becquerel was the first person to discover evidence of radioactivity.

Marconi and the radio

Italian scientist Guglielmo Marconi, working in England in the 1890s, pioneered a way of sending messages through the air using radio waves. Marconi used radio waves to transmit messages tapped out in Morse code. Because they travelled through the air and not along wires, as telegraph messages did, Marconi's messages could be sent vast distances, travelling around the world 'wireless'. Marconi's invention changed the way people communicated.

Marconi's first radio transmitter

Otto Lilienthal and the science of flight

In the 1860s German inventor Otto Lilienthal began studying aeronautics – the science of flight. Between 1891 and 1896, he put his research into practice in the form of a series of highly successful full-size glider trials, making close to 2,000 brief flights.

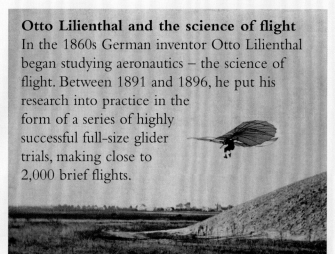

MODERN SCIENCE
SCIENCE OF THE SMALL

THE 20TH CENTURY SAW SOMETHING AS SMALL AS THE ATOM REVEAL ONE OF THE BIGGEST SCIENTIFIC DISCOVERIES OF ALL TIME – NUCLEAR ENERGY. LOCKED INSIDE THESE PARTICLES OF MATTER WAS AN ENERGY SOURCE OF UNBELIEVABLE POWER, WHICH SCIENTISTS DISCOVERED HOW TO RELEASE. IT WAS THE START OF THE NUCLEAR AGE.

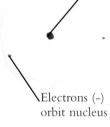

Nucleus made up of protons (+) and neutrons

Electrons (–) orbit nucleus

Rutherford's model of an atom

Electrons (–)

Thomson's model of an atom

Structure of the atom

Everything in the Universe is made from tiny particles of matter called atoms. Until 1897, scientists thought that atoms were the smallest particles, but that year British physicist John Thomson discovered that inside an atom were electrons, which are particles with a negative (–) electrical charge. The electron was the first subatomic particle, and it began to reveal the atom's structure.

In 1911, New Zealand-born physicist Ernest Rutherford found that an atom was mostly empty space. He said that at the centre of it was a tiny piece of matter, which he called the nucleus. Inside the nucleus was a subatomic particle with a positive (+) electrical charge, which he called a proton. In 1913 Danish physicist Niels Bohr discovered that electrons form shells or layers around the nucleus. In 1932 James Chadwick discovered the nucleus had a second subatomic particle – the neutron. Today more than 200 subatomic particles are known.

The 1930s and 1940s were exciting times for nuclear scientists, who were experimenting with nuclear fission, splitting the atom to release energy.

The nuclear age begins

Understanding the structure of the atom led to the nuclear age. In 1932, scientists at Cambridge University, England, split the atom by bombarding its nucleus until it fell apart. As the nucleus broke up, nuclear energy was released. It was a new energy source with awesome power. Scientists first used nuclear energy in 1945 to make atomic bombs, but since the 1950s it has been used to make electricity in nuclear power stations.

an artist's impression of the world's first man-made nuclear reactor, the Chicago Pile-1, in 1942

MODERN SCIENCE
ALBERT EINSTEIN

Albert Einstein, a German-born physicist, was perhaps the greatest scientist of the 20th century, and has been called a genius. His theories of relativity, which are about the behaviour of light, gravity and time, changed the way scientists thought about the Universe.

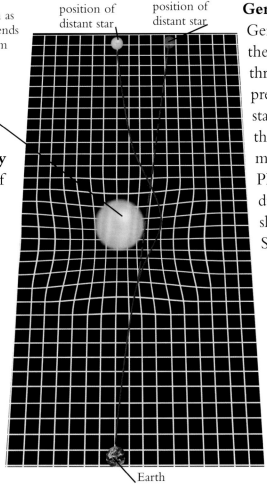

Sun's mass distorts space-time (shown as white grid) and bends light (red line) from distant star as if by a lens.

Actual position of distant star

Perceived position of distant star

Earth

Albert Einstein (1879–1955)

Einstein's theories of relativity

Einstein proposed two theories of relativity. The first theory was special relativity, published in 1905. It shows that time passes at different speeds for something moving very fast compared with something that is still – time slows down for things moving fast. Einstein's second theory was general relativity, published in 1915. It says that massive objects, such as stars, make space curve, causing light rays to bend. Both theories changed scientists' ideas about space and time.

General relativity (1915)

General relativity describes gravity and the way it affects light. Light travels through space in straight lines. Einstein predicted that as light passes close to a star, such as the Sun, it is forced by the star's gravity to bend – gravity makes the star behave like a lens. Photographs of stars taken before and during an eclipse showed them in slightly different places, proving the Sun's gravity had bent their light.

During a total eclipse in 1919, Arthur Eddington measured the positions of stars near the Sun and proved the Sun's gravity bent their light.

Special relativity (1905)

Einstein's theory of special relativity describes how the pace of time depends on how fast a person is travelling relative to something else. The theory predicts that time seems to run slowly on something moving at near the speed of light – about 300,000 kilometres (186,000 miles) per second – and that nothing can move faster than light. So, a beam of light inside a spaceship moving close to the speed of light would seem to travel farther to a person viewing it from the outside. Therefore time must have slowed down because the beam of light cannot go faster than the speed of light.

Mirror

Beam of light

Light source

Beam of light travels farther.

An observer on a spaceship travelling close to the speed of light sees a beam of light reflected back from a mirror to its source.

An imaginary observer outside the spaceship sees the path of the beam of light extended over a longer distance.

Because the speed of light is constant, time has to slow down to make up for the distance the light has travelled.

MODERN SCIENCE
SEEING THE INVISIBLE

Two scientists, working independently from each other in the 1920s, made one of the greatest discoveries in modern science – the Universe is expanding. This key discovery allowed a theory to be developed to explain the origins and age of the Universe itself – the Big Bang theory.

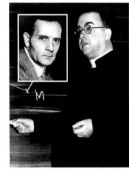

Hubble (inset) and Lemaître showed that the Universe is expanding.

Expanding Universe

Georges Lemaître (Belgium, 1927) and Edwin Hubble (USA, 1929) discovered that the Universe is expanding. They measured light reaching Earth from distant galaxies. They found the farther away a galaxy is, the faster it is travelling through space.

The Big Bang theory

In 1931 Lemaître put forward a new idea – that the Universe had started off as a single point in time. Since then, scientists have measured light reaching Earth fom the most distant galaxies. Knowing that light travels at a speed of about 300,000 km (186,000 miles) per second, they have tracked

At 305 metres (1,000 feet) across, the Arecibo Radio Telescope, Puerto Rico, is the world's largest dish antenna.

it back to the point at which it began its journey. By doing this they have calculated that the Universe began in an explosion 15 billion years ago. Called the Big Bang theory, it says energy released has been travelling through space and expanding the Universe ever since. In time, galaxies, stars and planets were formed.

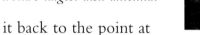

The Hubble Space Telescope, launched in 1990, took this image of the Orion nebula (left). The first photo of it, in 1880, (above) was by Henry Draper.

Electron microscopes

In the 1930s, German scientists invented a new type of microscope that used a beam of electrons to magnify an object's image. The electron microscope is much more powerful than an ordinary optical microscope, magnifying objects by up to a million times.

pollen, invisible to the eye, seen through an electron microscope

The Big Bang machine

The Large Hadron Collider (LHC) is the world's largest machine. Housed in a 27-km (16.8-mile) tunnel beneath the border of Switzerland and France, it began working in 2008. Two beams of protons, travelling at nearly the speed of light, are fired in oppositite directions around the tunnel. The beams collide head on, recreating the moment of the Big Bang and showing how the Universe appeared in the first microseconds of its existence.

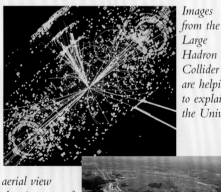

Images from the Large Hadron Collider are helping to explain the Universe.

aerial view showing part of the path of the underground Large Hadron Collider

MODERN SCIENCE
PLANET EARTH

IN THE 20TH CENTURY, SCIENTISTS TURNED THEIR ATTENTION TO A BETTER UNDERSTANDING OF PLANET EARTH. THEY CALCULATED ITS AGE AT SEVERAL BILLION YEARS OLD AND REALISED THAT THE CONTINENTS WERE ONCE ALL JOINED TOGETHER. THIS WORK HELPED TO EXPLAIN HOW ANCIENT LIFE HAD CROSSED BETWEEN LANDMASSES.

Alfred Wegener (1880–1930) was a German polar researcher, geophysicist and meteorologist.

Birth of the solar system

About 5 billion years ago, a group of stars were formed out of a cloud of gas and dust from the Big Bang. The stars slowly drifted apart. Some 4.6 billion years ago, gas and dust spinning around one of the stars – our Sun – started clumping together, forming planets, moons, asteroids and comets. It was the birth of the solar system.

Wegener noticed that the various landmasses seemed to fit together like a jigsaw puzzle, forming a single landmass. This super-continent has been given the name 'Pangaea', which means 'All Earth'.

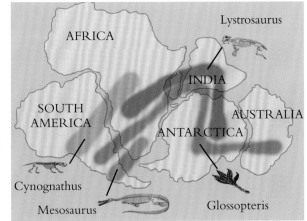

AFRICA

Lystrosaurus

INDIA

SOUTH AMERICA

AUSTRALIA

ANTARCTICA

Cynognathus

Mesosaurus

Glossopteris

Continents on the move

Until the early 20th century, scientists thought Earth's land had stayed much the same since the planet was born 4.6 billion years ago. This changed in 1915, when German scientist Alfred Wegener proposed the theory of continental drift, or plate tectonics. His idea was that all land was once joined up but split into pieces that moved across the planet to make today's continents. The continents are still moving, at up to 4 centimetres (1.6 inches) a year.

Fossil records

Wegener's theory solved the puzzle of why similar fossils were to be found on different continents. Land animals had simply walked across, long before the continents had moved apart.

From studying fossils of early man, Louis Leakey (1903–1972) proved that humans evolved in Africa.

Earth's atmosphere

In the 1860s, English balloonist James Glaisher made high-altitude ascents in a hot-air balloon, discovering the air got cooler the higher he went. By the end of the 19th century, French scientist Léon Teisserenc de Bort had found that above an altitude of 11 km (6.8 miles), the temperature ceased to fall and sometimes increased slightly. He named this upper part of the atmosphere the stratosphere. The lower part of the atmosphere, from the stratosphere down to sea level, he named the troposphere. Unlike the stratosphere, where the air is still, the air in the troposphere circulates, and it's where all of Earth's weather is created.

Léon Teisserenc de Bort (1855–1913) was the first to identify the troposphere and stratosphere.

A picture taken from space shows Earth's atmosphere. The orange layer is the troposphere, which gives way to the whitish stratosphere and then the blue mesosphere. Above that is the thermosphere.

MODERN SCIENCE
MEDICINE

THE ADVANCE OF MODERN SCIENCE HAS PERHAPS BEEN FELT MORE STRONGLY IN MEDICINE THAN IN ANY OTHER AREA OF LIFE. SCIENTISTS HAVE DEVELOPED MACHINES THAT CAN SEE INSIDE THE BODY, SURGEONS HAVE PERFORMED LIFE-SAVING TRANSPLANT OPERATIONS, MEDICINES HAVE FOUGHT OFF INFECTIONS AND THE BODY'S GENETIC CODE HAS BEEN MAPPED.

Czech scientist Jan Jansky is credited with the first classification of blood into the four types.

Blood types

In 1907, Jan Jansky classified human blood into four types – A, B, AB and O. His system is important to many medical procedures today, especially blood transfusions. It shows which blood type a person can receive, and is responsible for saving millions of lives.

Penicillin and the fight against infection

In 1928 Scottish scientist Alexander Fleming was at work in a hospital laboratory in London when he noticed that a susbstance coming from mould in a laboratory dish had killed bacteria next to it. He made one of the greatest breakthroughs in medical history. Fleming called the substance penicillin. He showed that it could be used to kill bacteria harmful to humans. In the 1940s a method of producing large amounts of penicillin was found, and more people than ever could be treated for infections caused by bacteria.

Alexander Fleming (1881–1955) discovered penicillin in 1928. In 1941 Howard Florey and Ernst Chain discovered how to mass produce it.

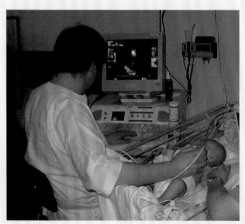

An ultrasound machine being used on a baby to check the internal organs, which appear as images on a monitor.

Seeing inside the human body

For about the first 60 years of the 20th century, X-ray images taken of the inside of the human body showed only the bones of the skeleton. Nothing could be seen of the organs or other soft tissue.

This began to change in the 1960s when ultrasound machines came into use. These produced images that could be used to investigate liver and heart problems, blood flow and show the health of a baby inside his or her mother.

A further advance came in the 1970s with the development of the computerised tomography (CT) scanner by British engineer Godfrey Hounsfield and South African-born physicist Allan Cormack. The CT scanner uses X-rays taken from many angles and a computer to create detailed images of the inside of the body – sometimes in three dimensions. CT scans are used to show injuries and problems with internal organs, helping doctors to decide on the best treatments.

Organ transplants

Since the mid-20th century surgeons have carried out increasingly complicated procedures to transplant human organs and body parts. The first such operation was in 1954, when a patient received a new human kidney. Since then, many other major organs have been successfully transplanted (lungs, heart, liver, pancreas and bowel). More recently, patients who have lost hands or suffered injuries to their faces have been able to receive transplants.

The perfusion pump, first made in 1935, keeps organs working when outside the body.

Christiaan Barnard (1922–2001) performed the first successful human heart transplant in 1967.

Towards understanding human genetics

One of the most important scientific discoveries of the 20th century came in 1953. British scientist Francis Crick, and James Watson from the United States, worked out the shape of a chemical called deoxyribonucleic acid (DNA). Found inside human genes, it's what makes each person unique.

Maurice Wilkins, Rosalind Franklin, James Watson, Francis Crick

DNA
double helix ———

Crick and Watson, working with X-ray photographs of DNA crystals taken by Maurice Wilkins and Rosalind Franklin, found that DNA was shaped like a twisted ladder, called a double helix (a spiral within a spiral).

This pioneering work in human genetics has led to an understanding of what is inherited from our parents. There are now possibilities of advances in medicine, as scientists find 'faulty genes' that cause diseases, and search for ways of controlling them. Because a person's DNA is unique to them, like a fingerprint, the police also use it to catch criminals.

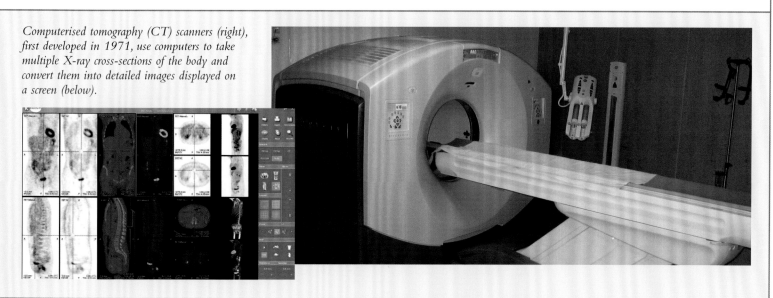

Computerised tomography (CT) scanners (right), first developed in 1971, use computers to take multiple X-ray cross-sections of the body and convert them into detailed images displayed on a screen (below).

GLOSSARY

alchemy
Early chemical science in which people (alchemists) studied chemicals and their reactions in an effort to change one substance into another.

alkali
A chemical substance that dissolves in water.

alpha rays
Stream of particles that are given off by radioactive substances.

alternating current
Electric current that flows first one way around a circuit, and then the other way. Alternating current is often abbreviated as AC.

astronomical
Relating to astronomy – the study of the Universe.

atmosphere
The layer of gases surrounding a planet.

atom
The smallest particle of an element, made up of a tiny nucleus at the centre surrounded by fast-moving electrons.

bacteria
Microscopic living organisms, some of which are dangerous to health, while others are beneficial.

beta rays
Stream of electrons that are given off by radioactive substances.

Big Bang
A theory about the origin of the Universe that says it began when something very small and hot exploded, causing it to expand, which it has been doing ever since.

biology
Study of living things (plants and animals).

chemical
Any substance that can change when joined or mixed with another substance.

chemistry
Study of matter (substances) and their properties.

direct current
Electric current that flows in one direction around a circuit. Direct current is often abbreviated as DC.

deoxyribonucleic acid
The chemical that makes up genes. It is often abbreviated as DNA.

electricity
A form of energy used for lighting, heating and making machines work.

electromagnetic spectrum
The complete range of electromagnetic radiation, measured in terms of waves, such as X-rays and radio waves.

electron
A tiny particle that travels around the nucleus of an atom.

electron microscope
A microscope that uses electron beams to produce greatly magnified images.

element
A substance made of one type of atom that cannot be broken down into any other substances.

galaxy
A group of millions or billions of stars.

gamma rays
Stream of particles given off by certain radioactive substances.

gravity
The force that attracts (pulls) two objects together.

lens
Curved piece of glass that brings light rays into focus.

light
Electromagnetic radiation that is visible to the eye, stimulating the sense of sight.

magnetic pole
One of two points on a magnet where the magnetic effect is strongest.

matter
Anything with mass that occupies space.

microscope
Scientific instrument that produces an enlarged image of an object through a system of lenses.

neutron
One of the two main particles found inside the nucleus of an atom.

nuclear energy
Energy released when the nucleus of an atom is split, or joined to another nucleus.

nucleus
Central part of an atom, made up of protons and neutrons.

periodic table
Chart with all the known chemical elements arranged in order, with similar ones together.

physics
Study of energy and forces.

plate tectonics
The idea that the surface of Earth is made from several large plates that are constantly on the move. Also known as continental drift.

proton
One of the two main particles found inside the nucleus of an atom.

radiation
Energy travelling as electromagnetic waves of particles. Heat, light and sound are types of radiation.

radioactivity
Breakdown of the nucleus of certain elements, causing radiation to be given off.

solar system
The Sun and the group of planets and other objects that orbit around it.

subatomic particle
Particle that is smaller than an atom, such as an electron or a proton.

ultrasound
A method of viewing images of inside the body with a machine that uses ultrasonic sound waves.

vaccination
Medical process that involves injecting a person to protect them against a particular disease.

wave
The way in which sound, light, heat and electricity travel.

wavelength
The distance between two peaks on a wave.

X-ray
An electromagnetic wave that can pass through certain materials, such as soft body tissue.

INDEX